MW01069625

Electric Dreams

THE ART OF

Barclay Shaw

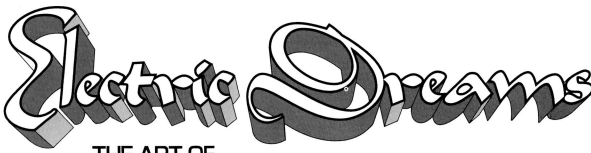

Electric Dreams

THE ART OF

Barclay Shaw

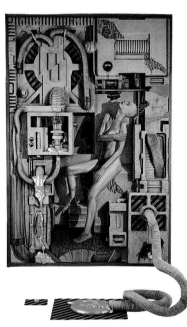

INTRODUCTION BY

Harlan Ellison

Paper Tiger

For my wife Kate and my children
Clay & Harrison

With special thanks to Harlan Ellison whose
boundless creative energy and extraordinary
willingness to try the unusual made this possible.

Paper Tiger
An imprint of Dragon's World Ltd
Limpsfield
Surrey RH8 0DY
Great Britain

© Dragon's World Ltd 1995
Introduction © The Kilimanjaro Corp. 1995
Illustrations & Text © Barclay Shaw 1995

CONTENTS

INTRODUCTION BY HARLAN ELLISON   6

EARLY WORK & SCULPTURE   10

THE ELLISON SERIES   18

WORKING METHODS   36

TECHNO SF & SPACE ART   40

FANTASY & SURREALISM   76

FUTURE MEDIA   122

▷ INSTALLATION

Chess Table sections are carefully carried up the spiral stairs in the office addition. Scaffolding is set up and the parts are lifted into place and assembled.

▽ CHESS TABLE IN PLACE

Harlan Ellison is seated, with his wife Susan in the doorway.

Although conceptually interesting, this piece is not intended to be suspended up in the air, as it seems here. A floor will be added to Mr. Ellison's office above the arched doorway at a later time. This will create a floor for the sole purpose of playing chess.

INTRODUCTION BY
Harlan Ellison

urely every philosopher since ancient Persia has had a go at describing Art. The size of Art; the shape of Art; the heft of Art and the burden of Art; the compulsion of Art and the great mystery of Art. Wonderful epigraphs and sparkling tropes. Picasso "A painting is a sum of destructions." Robert Smithson: "Establish enigmas. Not explanations." André Malraux: "All art is a revolt against man's fate." Incisive aphorisms and simply smashing metaphors. Susan Sontag: "Real art has the capacity to make us nervous." Yeah. Right. And according to Paracelsus, "man is coagulated smoke". All of which adds up to peanuts.

I sit here, twelve feet up a wall, waiting for the elf builders to come and put in a floor beneath my feet, and I contemplate the size, shape, heft, burden, compulsion, and great mystery of Art as proffered in the work of my long-time friend, Barclay Shaw. It is an expostulation I take upon myself in response to the elf publisher's request to "be inspired enough to write a nice introduction to Barclay's book" (29 March 95).

If every savant since Omar Khyyám has had his or her say as to the absolutely nifty matters of Art, well, so has every idiot. There is this anecdote about Whistler roaming incognito at a gallery showing of his work in London, sometime around 1863, and the great wit comes up behind this knot of society yokels who are held rapt by the observations of one self-important doyen who is sniffing down her aquiline snout at Whistler's paintings and saying, "I don't know what 'great Art' is… I only know what I like." At which point, Whistler taps her on the bustled ass with the ferrule of his walking stick, and when she turns he responds to her artistic insight thus: "That, madame, is a capacity shared by all forms of animal intelligence."

Whether insightful or idiotic, every Manny, Moe and Jack has an opinion on Art.

Am I "inspired enough" to be able to cobble together "a nice introduction" for my pal Barclay's first major volume of paintings? Hell, yes: but that is not the relevant question. All the inspiration I need to sing huzzahs over Barclay's talents is to wander through my own home, staring at the walls hung about with Shaw canvases.

But what is it all in aid of, save to put the lie to that old clinker about one picture being worth a thousand words? The dolt who coined that phrase, forever putting visual and verbal artists at each other's throats – strictly for the benefit of commercial slave-masters – ought to be forced to read all those hoary tomes about the nature of Art.

Inspiration is not the commodity necessary to get me to write about how excellently Barclay brings wonder and beauty into the world every day. What I need is an argument that holds water, that compels me to believe there is need for an introduction to a fine book of fine paintings. You see, this is not the first time I have been pressed thus into service. I have done it a number of times, because my own work has so often been enhanced by a liaison with Barclay's suave imagination.

For instance, in 1985, for some obscure pamphlet, I wrote: "Barclay Shaw is one of the most decent men I have ever met. He is a sweet man. Kind and gentle and fair and unassuming.

"The first time I saw one of his paintings, I bought it. It was clear to me that in a world where talent and vision are not as often welded as we might wish because there is never enough talent or vision to combat illiteracy, mediocrity, meanspiritedness and obscurantism), Barclay Shaw is a rara avis, an artist of truly remarkable capacities."

And then I went on to explain that while I have an absolutely breathtaking ability to conceive visual images in my mind (which, if impaired in any way, suffers only from my unseemly humility, a major character flaw that has held me back for donkey's years), I cannot draw for sour owl poop. Not even stick figures. So don't talk to me about frustration.

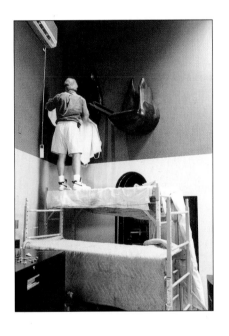

And I made it clear that my admiration for Barclay and his work is only partially a response to the high calibre of the work itself. The other measure of adoration proceeds from his uncanny, almost-telepathic link with my conceptual abilities. I tell him what I see, there on the perfect canvas of my inner eye, and Barclay makes it happen. He leaps it out into the real world.

Inspiration? I think not. I have a house filled with Barclay Shaw inspiration. Carved desks and organic chess tables that emerge from walls like Athena fullblown from the forehead of Zeus. Paintings of beasts that shout love at the heart of the world, and gentleman junkies, and venues with no doors, no windows. I don't need to be goosed to rave about the page after page of impeccable imaginings that have been assembled here.

All I need is a reason to believe that more words "about Art" will contribute even a scintilla of lustre to what Barclay dishes out on every one of these pages.

Poe-emz are writ by fools like me, but only Barc can paint a bleeding, eyeless, holy purple tree.

You're here now, so I commend your good sense to the owner of the manse, my friend and collaborator, the estimable Barclay Shaw. And when you get a chance, would you bring along a ladder? I think I need to use the facility.

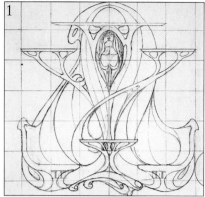

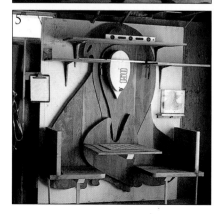

THE ELLISON CHESS TABLE

The construction of this piece took place over four years. When Harlan first called with the concept for the chess table, fashioned after the carved desk he purchased (see p. 17), I realized I was being given an extraordinary opportunity to create a truly unique and functional sculpture. Harlan's concept was so vivid that I had no trouble clearly envisioning the piece. I worked up a concept sketch (1) and small clay model (2) for Harlan's approval. Armed with the model, his comments, and photos of the installation location, I began work not only on construction considerations, but on how to physically get a 181 kg, 183 x 210 x 91 cm (72 x 80 x 36 in.) object up the narrow spiral stairs of Harlan's office addition.

We began by having three I-beams installed in Harlan's wall, just below seat and table level, not only to support the piece but to increase the likelihood of it remaining on the wall in the event of an earth quake. I then reproduced his wall in my studio and did a full size drawing on it (3). Walnut was selected as the material for the piece for its beauty and because its even grain carves nicely.

To solve installation problems, the piece was divided into seven units that would bolt together. This would also minimize environmental stresses that subtle changes in room temperature and humidity place on large masses of wood. The differences in density, moisture content, and grain within a single piece or between different pieces of wood can cause them to expand and/or contract at different rates, and produce splits, cracks, and other signs of stress.

The wood for the basic shapes was planed and glued, then cut according to paper patterns made from the full size drawing (4). I selected vermilion and figured maple for the chess board inlay.

After the basic units were fitted together and a drawer for taken chess pieces was made which straddled the supporting I-beam (6), I began to build up block lamination on each piece to achieve the necessary depth (7). This was a slow process, as each individual piece had to be glued then clamped for twenty four hours before the next piece could be added.

In the meanwhile, the central figure was modeled in clay over a styrofoam core. The clay figure was cast in plaster for the final carving (8), then shipped to the foundry to be cast in bronze. Patination was used on the bronze to subtly differentiate between flesh and hair.

With the lamination and fitting of the units complete, the rough carving of each piece was done with a chain saw (9). The final carving and sanding of the walnut units was done with a succession of power and hand tools. A finish of marine varnish was applied to minimize environmental effects.

The finished piece was assembled and photographed (10), then disassembled and shipped to Los Angeles.

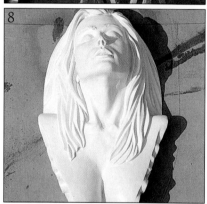

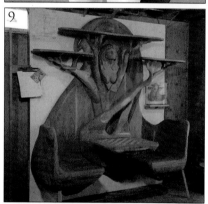

△ THE ELLISON CHESS TABLE
1991-1994
Walnut, Maple, Vermilion, and Bronze
183 x 210 x 91 cm (72 x 80 x 36 in.)
Functional sculpture, commissioned by
Harlan Ellison.

◁ ARTIST & WIFE
enjoy a quick game of chess before the
completed piece is shipped to Los Angeles.

INTRODUCTION   9

▽ DISMEMBERED COUCH
   W/ROTO-ROOTER CABLE 1972
Mixed Media
1.8 x 3 x 4.6 m (6 x 10 x 15 ft.)
Sculpture class project.

▽▽ ORGANIC CONSTRUCTION I
   1972
Mixed Media
2.4 x 3.6 x 3.6 m (8 x 12 x 12 ft.)
Sculpture class project.

EARLY WORK
&
SCULPTURE

To be able to work at a profession that is one and the same with the pursuit of one's muse is a true privilege in life, and I consider myself most fortunate to have found a career in the arts. Becoming established in a profession comes easily to some and is a struggle for others. It took me a while to settle upon a direction, let alone actively pursue one.

My painting and sculpture professors in college came directly from the New York City SoHo fine art scene, and taught art from that perspective. As was common in art education in the late Sixties and early Seventies, emphasis was placed on theory over art fundamentals and skill development, since the concept behind a piece was considered to be more important than the actual piece. Craftsmanship became incidental. In two years of painting classes, I may have attempted a mere three paintings on canvas. The rest of the time was spent stringing up canvas between buildings and the like.

I did develop a serious interest in sculpture while in college, although that was hard to tell from the art I produced then. I actually hauled the chopped-up fiberglassed couch pictured on this page (with Roto-Rooter cable) to an art show that was judged by the well known modern artist, Robert Motherwell, and won a sculpture prize for my efforts. This indicated to me not that there was something amiss with the standards of the contemporary fine art scene, but that here was a field one could enter with tongue firmly in cheek and easily succeed. However, after I presented a number of the local art galleries with the "dinosaur intestines" pictured here and was politely declined, I was forced to reconsider.

◁ OUTERSPACE III 1973
Watercolour on Illustration Board
56 x 71 cm (22 x 28 in.)
Poster for a rock band.

▽ MOUSE HOUSE 1974
Ink on Illustration Board
28 x 43 cm (11 x 17 in.)
Poster for a rooming house.

◁ OUTERSPACE IV 1973
Watercolour on Illustration Board
51 x 66 cm (20 x 26 in.)
Poster for a rock band.

The influence of the geometric constructions of Louise Nevelson, one of my favorite artists of that era, can plainly be seen on the cover of this book. My primary interest in art, however, was awakened by the psychedelic poster and underground comic movements of the late Sixties, and the Pre-Raphaelite and Art Nouveau movements that inspired them. When I seriously considered what I wanted to do with art at that time, it was to combine the fun I was having with abstract construction with the figurative art that I loved. But figurative art was out of vogue and no longer taught. In fine art circles, illustration was considered akin to prostitution, and I never considered it a viable option.

Rick Griffin was my favorite artist among the psychedelic underground, and I found myself copying his drawings in the margins of my college notebooks. After graduating from college with a most useful degree in Religion, I purchased an airbrush and taught myself to use it over a number of years. Some friends of mine had a rock-'n'-roll band, and my first paintings took the form of poster art for the band. The influence of Griffin is unmistakable in these posters (see p. 11). The hyper-real rendering style of Griffin appealed to me in its sculptural feel. He used a strong light source, a dark shadow, and clear reflected light, exaggerating the dimensionality of his work. His influence is still quite evident in my work today.

I held an assortment of non-art related jobs after graduating from college in 1972, but continued to work on more figurative sculpture (see below), and to experiment with the airbrush. I took a course in woodworking and began work on a functional sculpture desk, taking inspiration from the flowing organic forms of Art Nouveau furniture. I also found work in the woodworking field, but after a stint at a Boston furniture factory, I followed the example of a friend and fellow employee and enrolled in an art school in 1977 with an eye toward graphic design, a profession that was at least art related. I was a full-time art student for only a year, but was quite lucky in the assortment of instructors I had. Although my main course of study was design, I took basic art courses as well, and kept applying illustrative solutions to design problems (examples to the left). I had two illustration

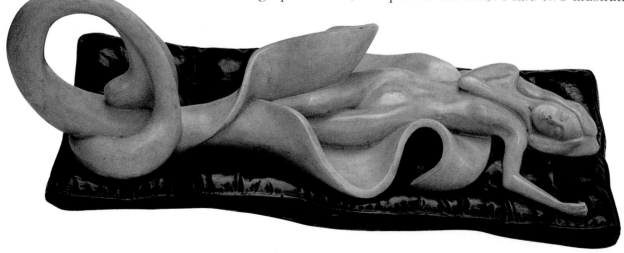

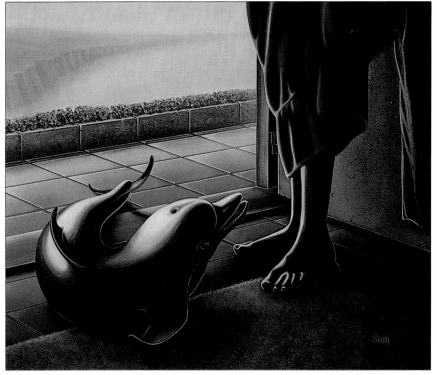

teachers who took fundamentally different approaches to technique: one tightly rendered, the other expressively loose and swashy. Together they provided an excellent balance to my instruction.

I was most fortunate to come across an illustration teacher, Bhob Stewart, who was active and quite well known in Science Fiction Fandom, although I had no idea what that was at the time. Bhob was not an instructor of mine when I first met him. I had always been interested in Science Fiction and was showing a spaceship I had just painted to someone in the school stairwell, when Bhob stopped to look at it. He said "This is good, you should do more." and walked off. I thought that was odd, but went home and did just that. When I showed him the results, he asked if he could send slides of the paintings to some magazines he wrote for. That secured my first professional assignments as an illustrator with The Magazine of Fantasy & Science Fiction and Cinéfantastique. In illustration I found a

△ INCUBUS 1979
Mixed Media
81 x 21 x 31 cm (32 x 8 x 12 in.)
Non-commissioned sculpture.

▷ DOLPHIN 1979
Acrylic
79 x 100 cm (31 x 40 in.)
Commissioned as interior art for Gallileo Magazine.

◁◁ SERIES PROGRESSION 1977
Watercolor on Illustration Board
79 x 100 cm (7 x 7 in.)
Art school project in design, showing a series progression in ten steps. The first and last panels of the series are shown.

◁ CE3K 1978
Watercolor on Illustration Board
79 x 100 cm (31 x 40 in.)
Commissioned as cover art for Cinefantastique.

◁◁ ORGANIC CONSTRUCTION III
1973
Mixed Media
81 x 21 x 31 cm (32 x 8 x 12 in.)
Non-commissioned sculpture.

EARLY WORK   13

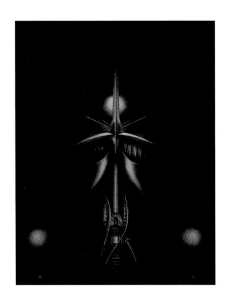

great balance between the need to follow the muse and the need to make a living.

It wasn't until after I had done my first few professional commissions that I began to combine brush work with airbrush work – quite the reverse of the way it is usually done. Up to this time I had been using watercolor inks on illustration board, sometimes adding pen work. When first experimenting with paint brushes and various media, I settled on acrylics because of their ease of use and compatibility (be it sometimes feisty) with the airbrush. The variety of textural effects produced when I actually began to paint was quite an awakening, oddly enough, and I was quickly able to achieve more professional results.

With my first few published pieces in hand, I approached other publications for freelance illustration work. Future Life magazine gave me an assignment a month at this time, giving me the opportunity to develop the discipline necessary for the business aspects of freelancing; for example providing sketches to specification, meeting tight deadlines, and making corrections on finished artwork.

△ CYBORG 1979
Acrylic
51 x 64 cm (20 x 25 in.)
Art school project, used as interior art for
Future Life Magazine.

▷ GATEKEEPER 1979
Acrylic
51 x 71 cm (20 x 28 in.)
Commissioned as cover art for The Magazine of
Fantasy & Science Fiction.

△ FUTURE EDUCATION 1979
Acrylic
56 x 100 cm (22 x 40 in.)
Commissioned as interior art for
Future Life Magazine.

▽ NOT THIS AUGUST 1981
Acrylic
51 x 71 cm (20 x 28 in.)
Commissioned as cover art for the 1981
TOR Books edition of **Not This August,**
by Frederick Pohl.

▷ ARTEMIS 1979
Acrylic
38 x 66 cm (15 x 26 in.)
Non-commissioned painting.
One of my first acrylic pieces.

▽ ELECTRIC SCULPTURE 1979
Mixed Media
38 x 31 x 31 cm (15 x 12 x 12 in.)
Non-commissioned sculpture, used as interior
artwork in Future Life Magazine.

The wonderful thing about doing Fantasy and Science Fiction painting is that although it is done within a strict editorial context, there is an enormous amount of artistic freedom in the subject matter. Because of the sometimes quite unusual nature of the subject matter unusual solutions might be accepted that would be anomalous elsewhere in the contemporary art world.

I will always enjoy doing sculpture, ranging from the funky to the functional. Working in clay is always physically satisfying, especially after working in the illusory 3D world of painting or computer modelling. Occasionally, I manage to integrate painting and sculpture in a medium relief, mixed media work. In the functional realm I recently completed a guitar synthesizer controller (see next page), and have a number of other more sculptural guitars in the works.

In 1980, after five years of intermittent work, I finally finished the Fantasy Desk. It was made from block laminated walnut and poplar, rough carved with a chain saw, and finished with hand and power tools. Needing to recoup some of the enormous amount of time and money spent on its construction, I took the desk to The 1980 World Science Fiction Convention held in Boston that year, and entered it in the art show for an initial bid that was below my cost for materials.

△ FANTASY DESK 1975-1980
Walnut and Poplar
91 x 122 x 122 cm (36 x 48 x 28 in.)
Non-commissioned functional sculpture; from
the collection of Harlan Ellison.

◁ GUITAR CONTROLLER 1994
Walnut, Maple Rosewood, and Hardware
100 x 31 x 7 cm (40 x 12 x 2.75 in.)
Non-commissioned MIDI guitar controller, for driving
synthesizer modules.

EARLY WORK   17

▷ SPIDER KISS 1981
Acrylic
51 x 71 cm (20 x 28 in.)
Commissioned as cover art for the 1982 Ace Books
edition of **Spider Kiss**, by Harlan Ellison.
▽ An alternate concept rough is below.

▽▽ STEELE WYOMING 1979
Acrylic
51 x 76 cm (20 x 30 in.)
Commissioned as cover art for The Magazine of Fantasy
& Science Fiction, from the collection of Harlan Ellison.

THE ELLISON SERIES

At the 1980 World Science Fiction Convention someone walked up to me and said that there was a bidding war going on over the fantasy desk (see p. 17) at the art auction. I walked in to find that the sculpture that I had hoped would sell for enough to reclaim my cost of materials had actually sold for enough to allow me to make a career move to New York City; and that it was purchased by none other than the author, Harlan Ellison. I later had the pleasure of meeting Harlan by my panel in the art show. He was interested in purchasing a painting titled Steele Wyoming. He liked the simplicity of the design and talked about using it as a design model for his series of books that were to be reprinted soon by Ace Books. He asked if I might be interested in illustrating them. Having only one book cover to my credit at that time, this was a unique opportunity, especially for someone just starting out. I was eager and willing to participate in the project.

With the proceeds from the desk sale, I moved to New York City, sharing a studio with a life-long friend who happened to be a photographer, quite an asset for an illustrator. In the meanwhile, during shipment to Los Angeles, the desk must have become overheated while in the back of the truck, probably while crossing the desert. The wood had split from having been forcibly dried by the heat, and the desk arrived literally in pieces. I was flown to LA at the carriers' expense to repair the damage. While there, Harlan and I discussed the overall design of his book series, and agreed on a unifying cover design using a graded wash background with a strong central figure or image. Simple, but effective. Harlan brainstormed for a while and came up with an image for the first book in the series, Spider Kiss, that was right up my alley: a rock star with a demon's face emerging from his guitar. I returned to home and began work on the painting.

▷ WEB OF THE CITY 1982
Acrylic
46 x 71 cm (18 x 28 in.)
Commissioned as cover art for the 1982 Ace Books
edition of **Web of the City**, by Harlan Ellison.
△ An alternate concept rough is above.

▷▷ LOVE AIN'T NOTHING 1982
Acrylic
46 x 71 cm (18 x 28 in.)
Commissioned as cover art for the 1982 Ace Books
edition of **Love Ain't Nothing But Sex Misspelled**,
by Harlan Ellison.

What I did not know was that authors rarely, if ever, have creative control over the design of their books. I walked into the offices of Ace Books and asked to see the art director. When asked if I had an appointment, I said that I had the cover painting for Spider Kiss. I sat down in the art director's office and after a moment he looked up and said: "You have the painting for Spider Kiss? We haven't assigned that book to an artist yet!" When I explained that the author had said that I had the job, he said that was not the way things were done. They would be selecting an illustrator for the series soon, but chances were good it wouldn't be me. I suggested that I leave

▷ PARTNERS IN WONDER 1982
Oil on Acrylic
46 x 71 cm (18 x 28 in.)
Commissioned as cover art for the 1983 Ace Books
edition of **Partners In Wonder**, by Harlan Ellison.
△ An alternate concept rough is above.

▷▷ GENTLEMAN JUNKIE 1982
Oil on Acrylic
46 x 71 cm (18 x 28 in.)
Commissioned as cover art for the 1983 Ace Books
edition of **Gentleman Junkie**, by Harlan Ellison.

the painting with him until a decision on the illustrator had
been made.

Harlan's powers of persuasion being what they are, I
received a call from the art director a while later, saying that the
painting wasn't too bad, really, and that they would like to use
me after all. Actually, Harlan does have cover approval in his
contracts, which in his case is an asset for all. He has an excellent innate sense of design, and it made my life quite easy.
I ended up doing a lot of preliminary sketches for the first
couple of paintings, trying to find an image that was satisfac-
tory to all involved. But after the first few paintings were

▷ NO DOORS, NO WINDOWS 1982
Oil on Acrylic
46 x 71 cm (18 x 28 in.)
Commissioned as cover art for the 1983 Ace Books
edition of **No Doors, No Windows**, by Harlan Ellison.

▷▷ I HAVE NO MOUTH 1982
Acrylic
51 x 76 cm (20 x 30 in.)
Commissioned as cover art for the 1983 Ace Books
edition of **I Have No Mouth And I Must Scream**,
by Harlan Ellison.

completed, Ace Books was confident enough in Harlan's and my ability to create successful cover art that they gave it all over to us. The working method was straightforward. On the phone, Harlan would brainstorm ideas (never any shortage there), and we would select among them and discuss the visual editing necessary to fit the series format. I would then send comprehensive sketches to Harlan for comment, and after final approval from Ace Books, I would execute the final painting.

One part of the series that did not proceed quite as smoothly as others was THE GLASS TEAT and THE OTHER GLASS TEAT. The initial concept was to have one painting for both

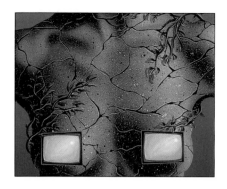

▷ GLASS TEAT SCULPTURE 1986
Mixed Media
274 x 76 x 61 cm (7 x 2.5 x 2 ft.)
Non-commissioned sculpture, shown in *off* and
on conditions.

▷▷ THE GLASS TEAT 1982
Acrylic
46 x 71 cm (18 x 28 in.)
Commissioned as cover art for the 1983 Ace Books
edition of **The Glass Teat**, by Harlan Ellison.
△ An alternate concept rough is above.

▽ THE OTHER GLASS TEAT 1982
Oil on Acrylic
46 x 71 cm (18 x 28 in.)
Commissioned as cover art for the 1983 Ace Books
edition of **The Other Glass Teat**, by Harlan Ellison.

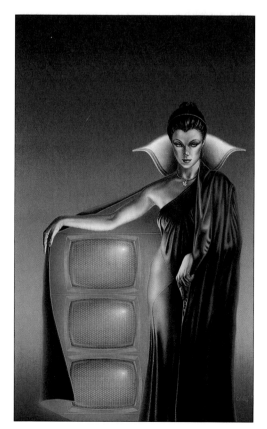

titles: the left half for one and the right for the other. When
the books were racked side by side in the book stores, the
original painting would be recreated. Ace books was a
little put off by the image of TV breasts (see above), and
we went with a different concept. I, of course, found the
first concept irresistible and a few years later constructed a
large (and as you can see, quite tasteful) interactive sculpture based on the idea. It had a motion sensor installed at
the very top, which would cause the base to light up when
the sculpture was approached. A tape recorded voice
would then ask the viewer to touch a contact switch in the
sculpture's middle, which would light up after the record-
ing ended. The upper front section of the sculpture was
faced with a one-way mirror, reflecting the viewer. When
the contact switch was touched, the interior of the top
section would light up, revealing a female torso with TV
breasts. I had planned to install a closed circuit TV camera
so that that viewer would be displayed in the televisions,
but never quite got around to it.

In some instances an artist is called upon to make fairly
major changes to a painting. The reasons can include
design considerations such as colour, the value (lightness
or darkness) of an area, or placement of image elements,
perhaps with a view to their overall composition including
typography. Other reasons range from editorial considerations to pure whim. In the case of PAINGOD, it was
image content, plain and simple. When I submitted the
first version of the painting (see p. 28) to Harlan and Ace

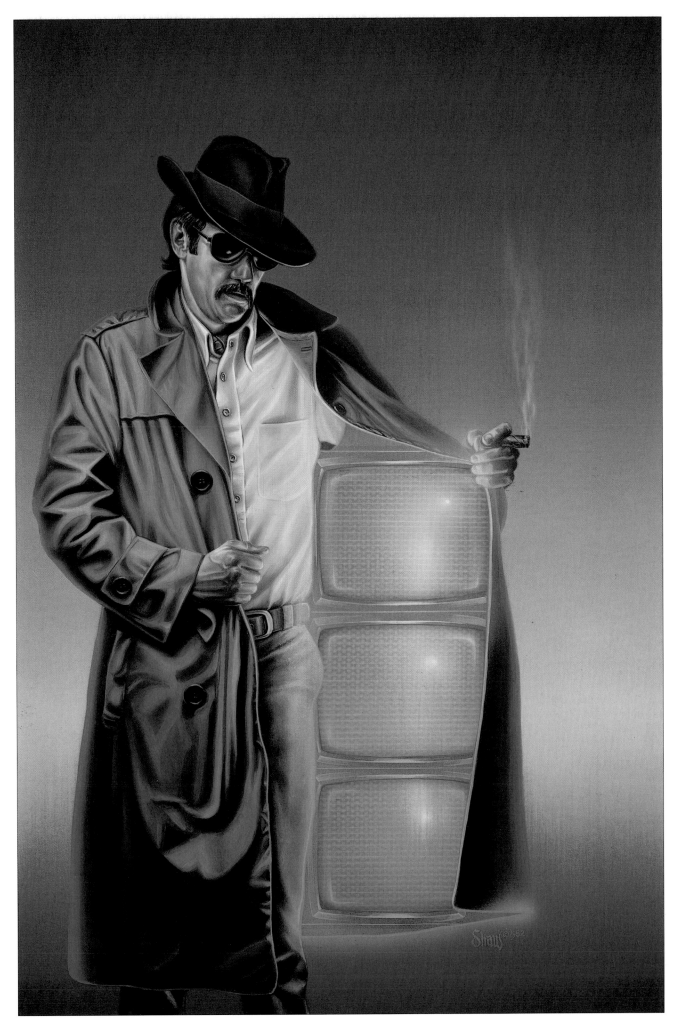

▷ First version of **Paingod**.

▷▷ PAINGOD 1983
Acrylic
46 x 71 cm (18 x 28 in.)
Commissioned as cover art for the 1984 Ace Books
edition of **Paingod**, by Harlan Ellison.

Books, they were unanimous in their response: androgynous
or not, cover that figure! So with a small brush in hand and
many, many feathers later, we had an acceptable painting. The
shock value was intended to be high, but the first version was
admittedly a bit much. This is actually an example of good
art direction. The excesses of the artist were held in check and
the overall image was improved. The revised version retains the
impact of the first, while making a much more acceptable
cover for the book store shelves.

The time given to complete each piece in the series varied
considerably, usually from about a month to as little as a few

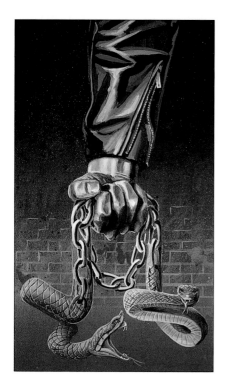

▷ MEMOS FROM PURGATORY 1983
Oil on Acrylic
51 x 76 cm (20 x 30 in.)
Commissioned as cover art for the 1984
Ace Books edition of **Memos From Purgatory**,
by Harlan Ellison.

▷▷ THE DEADLY STREETS 1983
Oil on Acrylic
46 x 71 cm (18 x 28 in.)
Commissioned as cover art for the 1984 Ace Books
edition of **The Deadly Streets**, by Harlan Ellison.
△ The colour concept rough is above.

days. This is determined by a variety of factors. Production schedules generally determine the time given, but the more people involved in the approval process, for example, the more likely delays will occur, which cuts directly into execution time for the artist. The challenge for the artist comes in the need to maintain consistent quality in the work under varying circumstances. Working on this series with all the different artistic and business factors provided a real education for this artist.

There were twelve titles in the Ace Books reprint series. Bluejay Books, under publisher and editor Jim Frenkel, picked up an additional four titles in the series and produced trade editions of those. Jim paid an enormous amount of care and attention to every aspect of his business and produced a line of books of outstanding quality. In an unusual act of faith for an editor, he

▷ DEATHBIRD STORIES 1983
Acrylic
51 x 71 cm (20 x 28 in.)
Commissioned as cover art for the 1984 Bluejay
Books mass market edition of **Deathbird Stories**,
by Harlan Ellison.

▷▷ THE BEAST 1983
Acrylic
51 x 71 cm (20 x 28 in.)
Commissioned as cover art for the 1984 Bluejay
Books edition of **The Beast That Shouted Love
At The Heart Of The World**, by Harlan Ellison.
△ The concept rough is above.

allowed Harlan and I to continue our working methods on the series. During the brainstorming session for THE BEAST THAT SHOUTED LOVE AT THE HEART OF THE WORLD (right), Harlan shouted: "I've got it! A cherub is shot by an arrow and falls on an egg shaped Earth – only, instead of yoke, blood leaks out of the cracks in the egg!".

After the rough was approved, the editor's child cheerfully modelled for the wounded cherub in the final painting. Good reference materials are most helpful for an illustrator, and I generally use models whenever possible. My wife for example, in her NYC combat fatigues, modelled for APPROACHING OBLIVION (see p. 35).

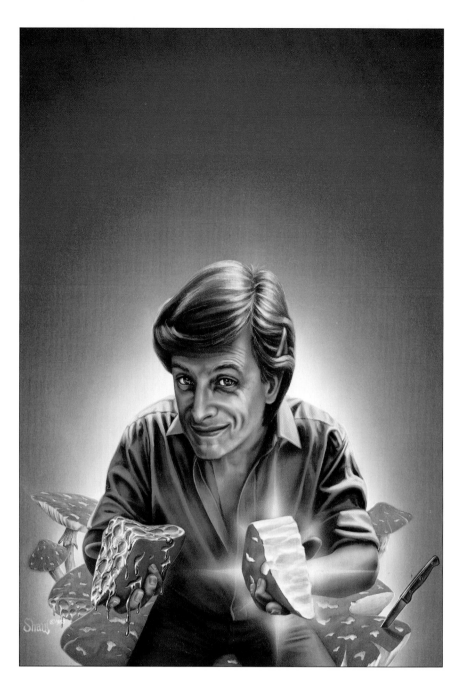

▷ ELLISON WONDERLAND 1984
Oil on Acrylic
51 x 71 cm (20 x 28 in.)
Commissioned as cover art for the 1985 Bluejay Books
edition of **Ellison Wonderland**, by Harlan Ellison.

▷▷ APPROACHING OBLIVION 1984
Acrylic
56 x 36 cm (22 x 34 in.)
Commissioned as cover art for the 1985 Bluejay Books
edition of **Approaching Oblivion**, by Harlan Ellison.

In a tip of the hat to Leo and Diane Dillon, the artists to first illustrate the Ellison series and who included Harlan's image in each painting, a number of my paintings for the series also include Harlan's image; I HAVE NO MOUTH & I MUST SCREAM (p. 25) being notable among them. Working on this series and other projects with Harlan has been one of the true joys of my professional life. Harlan's enthusiasm for the arts has not only been instrumental in shaping my career and development as an artist. His artistic interest and patronage continually expand to include artists across an amazingly broad spectrum of styles, areas of interest, and media. Harlan is sincerely appreciated for it.

▽ The artist's studio.

▽ ▽ A removable venting hood that, when attached
to the drafting table, catches and removes airbrush
over-spray mist.

WORKING METHODS

tudios of artists are usually interesting in one way or another, and are always revealing of the individual. In my studio, pictured here, art materials can be found in equal measure with art books (filling the entire right wall, which is out of view) and assorted electronics. Being disorganized of mind, I have to keep the studio well organized. With so much stuff around, a misplaced item can be lost for years.

Also pictured here is an innovation developed over years of airbrush use: a custom hood that attaches to my drawing table and acts like a spray booth to remove airbrush over-spray. It is designed to fit over my standard size paintings, but also can rest on a portion of a large painting, and so can accommodate practically any size work. There is an external vacuum blower with ducting into the studio, which can be switched on and off from the art table. A flexible hose connects the ducting to the hood, and the whole thing can be set up or removed in seconds.

Since so much time is spent in the studio, I find that a comfortable environment that is conducive to work helps when the inclination may be lacking, and a deadline must be met. I like to listen to music while drawing and painting, and especially when working at the computer. While doing time-consuming rendering on a painting, full length readings of books on audio cassette are great! It is like having someone sitting in your studio reading to you while you paint.

The working procedures for illustration vary slightly by the type of assignment. In advertising, the client provides the artist with a comp, or rough drawing to size, of the desired image. The artist then does his own tighter pencil drawing of the image, and then the full painting, according to comments on the sketch by the client. In editorial illustration, there tends to be a bit more creative freedom. The artist is generally first sent the manuscript to read. The artist will do a few pencil drawings of different ideas derived from the text. The art director will choose among the pencil roughs, and the artist will then do a more detailed version of the selected concept, sometimes in colour. On approval, the artist will then do the final painting. In editorial work, even if the art directors or editors request a specific image or scene, there is generally great latitude given in the ways the artist can approach the image. In advertising, elements are usually locked into a tight layout, with little or no latitude for variation.

To the right is a collection of preliminary sketches done for MINING THE OORT. Of the five concepts, only one is black and white, because I sometimes prefer to visualize in colour, given enough time. The concept at the far right was selected by the art director, with minor changes in view angle and layout requested.

Having good reference for a painting can make all the difference. To help work out light and shadow areas in perspective on a painting element, I will sometimes build a small clay model and throw a light source on it to use as reference, like the alien to the right. Computer modelling now makes it much easier to work out more complex perspective and lighting situations realistically. For figure reference, I will sometimes photograph professional models if the client has the budget for it. Otherwise I may recruit friends, family, or acquaintances for the task. I have even called family pets into service, but not for the reasons implied by the brush illustration.

For roughing in a painting, I use mostly larger flat, bright, and filbert brushes with the acrylics thinned, to minimize the paint thickness. With the entire painting brushed in, I will sometimes use the air-brush to add atmospheric effects if needed, and to model elements of the painting, which increases the illusion of depth. Detailing brush work is done with small watercolour rounds or brights. I use thinned acrylics for the detail work too, unless thicker paint is needed for drybrush effects. Acrylic retarder is useful in extending drying times in areas that require extensive blending. I frequently use oil paint over acrylic where subtle colour and smooth blending are needed.

For painting surfaces I seem to vacillate between illustration board, stretched canvas, and canvas board. The properties of each vary, and I choose whichever will best suit the job. I have the most fun experimenting with different combinations of paints, materials, and now digital media.

△△△ A collection of roughs done for **Mining The Oort** (see p. 74).

△△ A clay reference model, sculpted for **The Remaking of Sigmund Freud** (see p. 91).

△ A selection of brushes used by the artist.

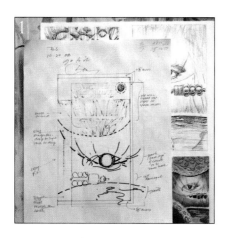

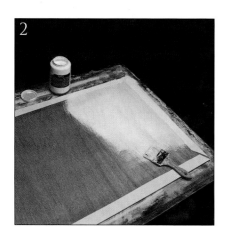

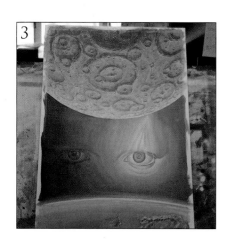

1.) The first step to any illustration is the preliminary sketch. Pictured here are a number of my roughs, pencil and colour. The art director's comments are shown on a tracing paper overlay placed over a pencil sketch.

2.) The painting surface is prepared. I usually paint on illustration board or canvas. In this case it is canvas glued over 5 mm luan plywood with archival paste. Gesso is applied to both sides of the panel to minimize warping. I usually apply three coats, sanding in between each coat. The drawing is then transferred to the panel in pencil.

3.) Next, I brush in the entire painting, using thinned acrylics and relatively large brushes. I use a muffin tray to hold the mixed paint. Values and colours are established, with some areas more tightly rendered than others, depending on the amount of airbrush modelling to be done or whether an additional element is to be painted over an area later.

4.) Each area that I want to apply airbrush modelling to is masked off and sprayed. I use a vinyl friskit paper, cut with a razor knife. I usually use dark transparent colours for rounding or tinting an object, and opaque light colours for highlights or atmospheric effects.

5.) If an object is to be placed over a background element, like the spaceship here, I will sometimes completely render the entire background first, then paint the foreground element over it, following the same procedure.

6.) I will go back in with the airbrush to further model the form of the new element, and to add highlights as needed. French curves are indispensable for controlling spray within an area masked with friskit.

7.) I then go back in on the whole painting with a brush to add detailing, or to bring out elements or textures that were subdued by airbrushing. I am using a ruler here, slightly raised from the surface, to rule a straight line with a brush. It is at this point that I will add oil paint to the process if called for. I find oils especially useful for smooth skin tones, which are difficult to achieve in acrylic because of its quick drying time. Oils will adhere nicely to acrylics (but not the other way). When complete, the painting is sprayed with a protective coat of MSA acrylic varnish that goes over both oil and acrylic paint beautifully.

8.) When airbrushing, even when using an over-spray removal system, it is important to use some sort of face mask or respirator. Introducing some of the paint chemicals into the body through the respiratory system is not only a fine way to reduce the number of those harmful brain cells, but can contribute to an early retirement for the lungs.

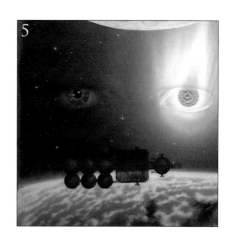

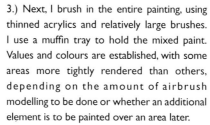

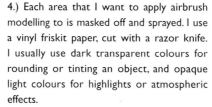

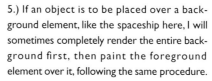

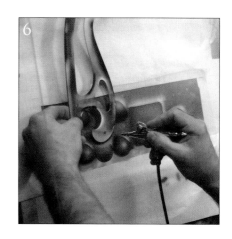

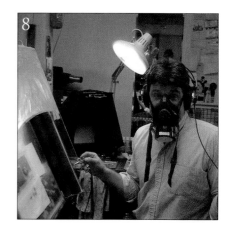

▷ MERCHANTER'S LUCK 1982
Oil on Acrylic
46 x 71 cm (18 x 28 in.)
Commissioned as cover art for the 1983 DAW Books
edition of **Merchanter's Luck**, by C. J. Cherryh.

▽ SENTENCED TO PRISM 1985
Acrylic
46 x 71 cm (18 x 28 in.)
Commissioned as cover art for the 1986 Ballantine
Books edition of **Sentenced To Prism**, by A. D. Foster.

▽▽ UPWINGERS 1982
Acrylic
38 x 63 cm (15 x 25 in.)
Commissioned as interior art for Future Life Magazine.

TECHNO SF & SPACE ART

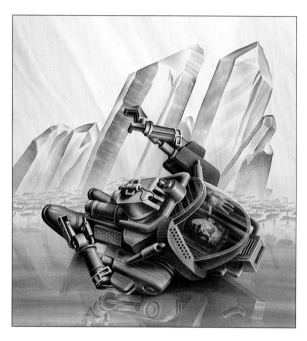

Beginning with the earliest Science Fiction literature, fantastic illustrations have always complemented the writing, and have become an integral part of the genre. While growing up, I read mostly Science Fiction and Fantasy stories for entertainment, and was captivated by the artwork just as much as by the stories. As an adult I have found myself in the privileged position of illustrating some of the very same, and now classic, Science Fiction and Fantasy stories.

There is an aspect of illustration that is, in a sense, a participation in the communication of the story being illustrated; in the same way that a musician participates in the musical communication of a written score by playing it. And like the musician, the artist can bring a piece of himself to the existing work, participating in and adding to its message. Being a part of the pleasure produced by good literature, classic or new, is one of the joys of illustration. If some of that joy is transmitted to the viewer through the artwork, the artist has excelled at his task.

One glance at my studio (see p. 36) will inform the viewer that technology holds a certain allure for me. It is, after all, a driving and sustaining force in our current society, for good or ill. Consequently elements of technology can make excellent cultural symbols. Like any human tool, technology is morally neutral, its use and impact being determined by its user. But it can take on tremendous symbolic weight. Atomic energy in the Fifties, for example, was touted as both the saviour and destroyer of society. Because the economy of our society is supported by technology, we are on one hand inseparable from it. On the other hand, there is the aspect of the human soul that soars above any of the works of man. Here is an infinite resource for the arts. As in the two paintings on this page,

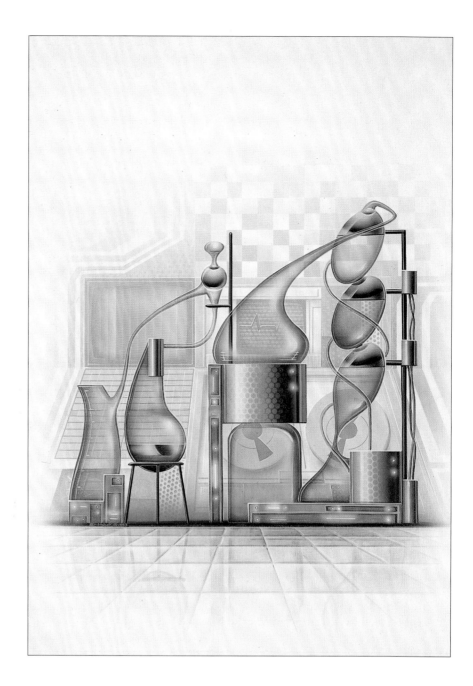

▷ HEALER 1982
Acrylic
46 x 71 cm (18 x 28 in.)
Commissioned as cover art for the 1983 Ace Books
edition of **Healer**, by F. Paul Wilson.

▷▷ DR. ADDER 1983
Oil on Acrylic
51 x 71 cm (20 x 28 in.)
Commissioned as cover art for the 1984 Bluejay
Books edition of **Dr. Adder**, by K. W. Jeter.

▽ SCAPESCOPE 1984
Acrylic
46 x 71 cm (18 x 28 in.)
Commissioned as cover art for the 1984 Ace Books
edition of **Scapescope**, by John Stith.

mankind could be mortally trapped by its technology, or freed by it. I love to paint all aspects of technology: from malevolent tech, to "Bright Future" tech, to simple benign clutter. Juxta-posing or combining technology with the figure, be it human or alien (a human symbol), is cause for celebration.

Elements in Space Art are just as adaptable as those of tech-nology, in that space is similarly neutral and can have any mantle placed upon it. Even if a Space Art painting is informed by hard science, it can have qualities such as beauty, porten-tousness, or wonder imposed upon it. The fact that technology is a requirement for space exploration makes them inseparable, and part of the same visual language. Some of the best illustra-tion of our time is far more reflective of the attitudes, fears, and dreams of our society than is much of contemporary academic fine art, and may be seen as such by future art historians. But keep in mind that an illustrator said that.

△△ CROSS-TIME ENGINEER 1988
Acrylic
46 x 71 cm (18 x 28 in.)
Commissioned as cover art for the 1989 Ballantine
Books edition of **The Cross-Time Engineer**,
by Leo Frankowski.

△ RADIANT WARRIOR 1988
Acrylic
46 x 71 cm (18 x 28 in.)
Commissioned as cover art for the 1989 Ballantine
Books edition of **The Radiant Warrior**,
by Leo Frankowski.

△ VOYAGE TO THE
   CITY OF THE DEAD 1984
Acrylic
46 x 71 cm (18 x 28 in.)
Commissioned as cover art for the 1989 Ballantine
Books edition of **Voyage To The City Of The Dead**,
by Alan Dean Foster.

▷ AGENTS OF INSIGHT 1985
Acrylic
46 x 71 cm (18 x 28 in.)
Commissioned as cover art for the 1986 TOR Books
edition of **Agents of Insight**, by Steven Klaper.

△ DOOR INTO SUMMER 1985
Oil on Acrylic
46 x 71 cm (18 x 28 in.)
Commissioned as cover art for the 1986
Ballantine Books edition of **Door Into Summer**,
by Robert A. Heinlein.

▷ THE RED PLANET 1989
Acrylic
46 x 71 cm (18 x 28 in.)
Commissioned as cover art for the 1989
Ballantine Books edition of **The Red Planet**,
by Robert A. Heinlein.

▷▷ WALDO & MAGIC INC. 1986
Oil on Acrylic
46 x 71 cm (18 x 28 in.)
Commissioned as cover art for the 1986
Ballantine Books edition of **Waldo & Magic Inc.**,
by Robert A. Heinlein.

Problem solving is a primary, and quite enjoyable component of illustration. It was a happy day when I was given five classic Robert Heinlein novels to illustrate. When I received the assignment, however, I was asked to continue the ellipse motif found in the background of artist Michael Whelan's extraordinarily powerful cover painting for Heinlein's FRIDAY. This was not a request to copy another artist's work, but a challenging exercise in problem solving. It is important for a publisher to be able to maintain a consistent look on a book series, even if different artists are used on the series.

▷ DOUBLE STAR 1986
Oil on Acrylic
46 x 71 cm (18 x 28 in.)
Commissioned as cover art for the 1986
Ballantine Books edition of **Double Star**,
by Robert A. Heinlein.

▷▷ PUPPET MASTERS 1986
Oil on Acrylic
46 x 71 cm (18 x 28 in.)
Commissioned as cover art for the 1986
Ballantine Books edition of **The Puppet Masters**,
by Robert A. Heinlein.

The problem was how to continue the ellipse motif while at the same time creating a unique and appropriate image for each book, and allowing a different artist's voice to come through. Among the different cover solutions, my favourite is the painting for THE PUPPET MASTERS (right). The figure and perspective are interesting and the image was a lot of fun to create, from drawing to painting. The marbling was done by wetting part of the surface, then dripping thinned acrylic paint onto it. A hair dryer is useful for drying acrylics and for blowing wet paint around to achieve different textures.

▷ ASCENDENCIES 1984
Oil on Acrylic
46 x 71 cm (18 x 28 in.)
Commissioned as cover art for the 1984 Ace Books
edition of **Ascendencies**, by D. G. Compton.

▷▷ CAT'S GAMBIT 1989
Oil on Acrylic
61 x 100 (24 x 40 in.)
Commissioned as cover art for the 1989 Ballantine
Books edition of **Cat's Gambit**, by Leslie Gadallah.

▷ NEUROMANCER 1986
Oil on Acrylic
730 x 100 cm (288 x 40 in.)
Commissioned as cover art for the 1986 Phantasia
Press edition of **Neuromancer**, by William Gibson.

▷ A concept rough for an expanded version of the
painting is below.

EUROMANCER was a
ground breaking book, introducing cyberspace first to SF literature, then to the culture at large. In the painting, the reflection
of cyberspace in the drug store window integrates it into the
anarchistic street scene. The expanded watercolour sketch to
the right was for a mural sized version of the painting, which
would incorporate three dimensional elements into the two
dimensional painting.

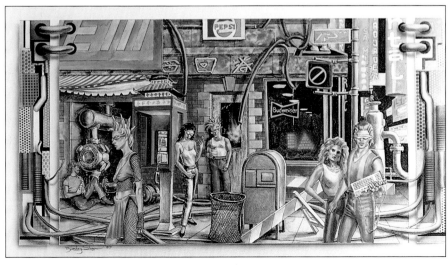

▷ THE BEST OF
  JOHN BRUNNER 1988
Oil on Acrylic
43 x 66 cm (17 x 26 in.)
Commissioned as cover art for the 1988 Ballantine
Books edition of **The Best Of John Brunner**.

▷▷ ILLEGAL ALIEN 1989
Oil on Acrylic
46 x 71 cm (18 x 28 in.)
Commissioned as cover art for the 1990 Ballantine
Books edition of **Illegal Alien**, by James Luceno.

▷ TEXAS ON THE ROCKS 1985
Acrylic
43 x 66 cm (17 x 26 in.)
Commissioned as cover art for the 1986
Ballantine Books edition of **Texas On The Rocks**,
by Daniel da Cruz.

A sizable iceberg is being delivered under duress to The Federal Republic Of Texas to alleviate a water shortage.

▷▷ DIVERGENCE 1990
Acrylic
51 x 87 cm (20 x 34 in.)
Commissioned as cover art for the 1990 Ballantine
Books edition of **Divergence**, by Charles Sheffield.

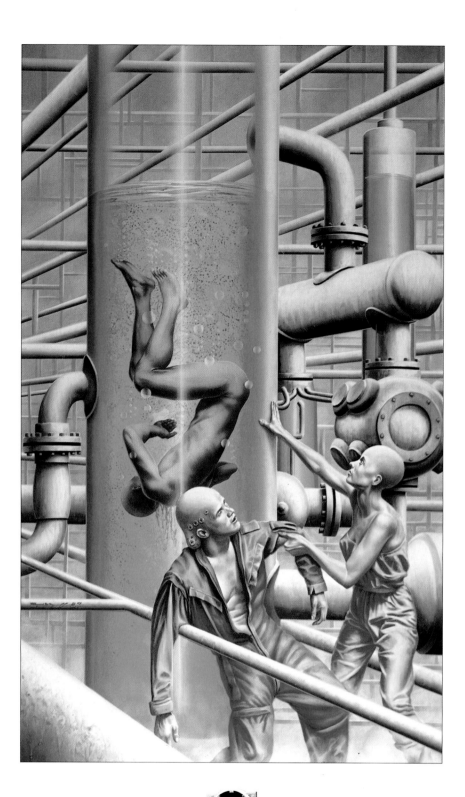

▷ CORPSEMAN 1987
Acrylic
46 x 71 cm (18 x 28 in.)
Commissioned as cover art for the 1987 Ballantine
Books edition of **Corpseman**, by Joel Sherman.

▷▷ F CUBED 1986
Oil on Acrylic
46 x 71 cm (18 x 28 in.)
Commissioned as cover art for the 1987 Ballantine
Books edition of **F Cubed**, by Daniel da Cruz.

One can never have enough tubes, pipes and ductwork in this life, in my opinion. I enjoy technological clutter because it at least brings to mind mechanical versions of the different bodily systems, like the respiratory or circulatory systems, or nerve networks and so on. It can reflect the different conditions of the body from young and new to old and corroding. It can also contain wonderful contrasts between rigid linear elements like tubing, and more flowing free-form, but still mechanical, elements like flexible hoses. Contrast this with a truly fluid organic form, human for example, and you are cookin' with gas.

▷ SUPERCONDUCTIVITY 1987
Oil on Acrylic
76 x 100 cm (30 x 40 in.)
Commissioned as interior art for The Weekly Reader,
Field Publications.

This is an illustration incorporating many of the possible
future uses for superconductivity. Two accompanying
diagrams are below. The left illustrating electron flow
through a normal power line, the right through a
superconducting line.

▷▷ HOMEGOING 1988
Acrylic
56 x 92 cm (22 x 36 in.)
Commissioned as cover art for the 1989 Ballantine
Books edition of **Homegoing**, by Frederick Pohl.

▽ GOLDEN FLEECE 1990
Acrylic
61 x 100 cm (24 x 39 in.)
Commissioned as cover art for the 1990 Warner
Books edition of **Golden Fleece**, by Robert J. Sawyer.

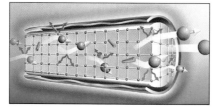 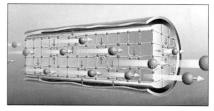

Space art and surrealism
are natural companions to each other, but are infrequently
combined. In order to give Space Art its sense of verisimilitude
it must be painted as though the painting were a photograph of
an existing reality. But actually Space Art is often a juxtaposition
of recognizably real and fantastic elements that create a mood
or statement that goes well beyond the elements themselves,
and can be fundamentally surrealist in nature. For Space Art to
have overtly surrealist elements would disrupt its illusion of
reality. But that is why I love it when it does! HOMEGOING
(right), ASCENDENCIES (see p. 50), and UPWINGERS (see
p. 40) are examples where I have done this.

▷ DOWNTIMING
    THE NIGHT SIDE 1992
Acrylic
46 x 71 cm (18 x 28 in.)
Commissioned as cover art for the 1993 Baen
Books edition of **Downtiming The Night Side**,
by Jack Chalker.

*The multiple overlapping images create a montage approach
to time travel.*

▷▷ SHOCKWAVE RIDER 1988
Acrylic
46 x 71 cm (18 x 28 in.)
Commissioned as cover art for the 1989 Ballantine
Books edition of **Shockwave Rider**, by John Brunner.

*This is a symbolic depiction of the electronically induced
multiple realities contained in the text.*

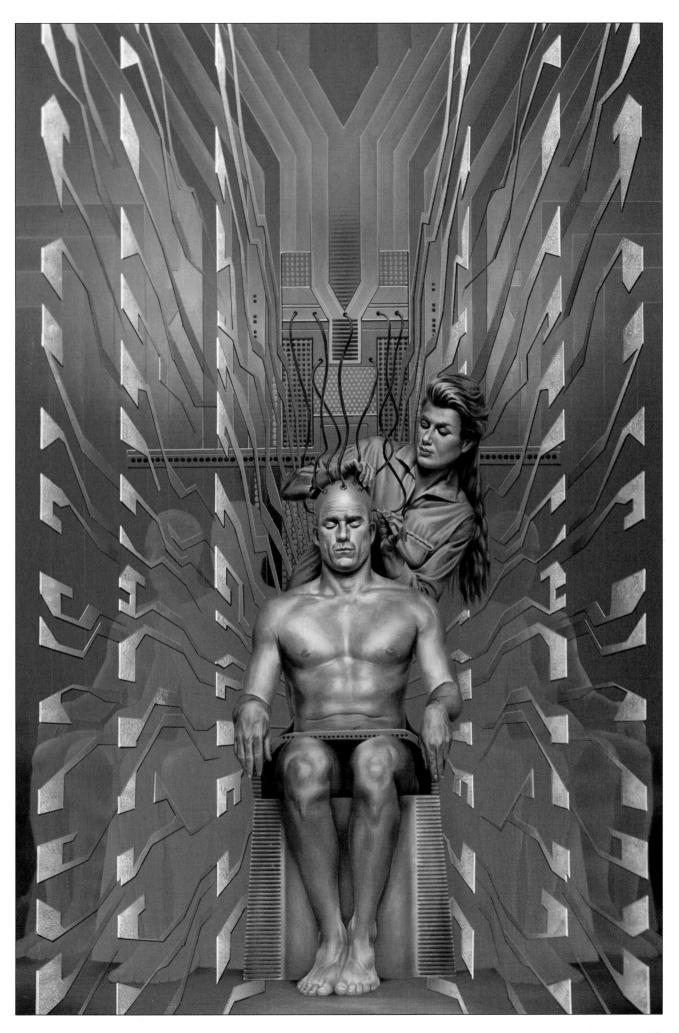

◁◁ WORLD AT THE
(p. 64) END OF TIME 1989
Oil on Acrylic
61 x 100 cm (24 x 39 in.)
Commissioned as cover art for the 1990 Ballantine
Books edition of **The World At The End Of Time**,
by Frederick Pohl.

*The exaggerated perspective of this piece is used to
illustrate the speed and distance travelled by the planet
and its solar system, after it has been propelled so far out
toward the edge of the universe that no other stars are
visible excepting its own sun.*

◁ (p. 65) SUBWAY LOVE 1988
Mixed Media
122 x 183 x 25 cm (4 x 6 ft. x 10 in.)
Non-commissioned medium relief sculpture, used as
cover art for the 1989 Ballantine Books edition of
Kaleidoscope, by Harry Turtledove.

*This is the first in a series of mixed media, medium relief,
painting/sculptures.*

▷ TOTAL ECLIPSE 1989
Acrylic
76 x 100 cm (30 x 40 in.)
Commissioned as cover art for the 1990 Warner
Books edition of **Total Eclipse**, by John Shirley.

*The scene is of war-torn near-future Europe, where the
New Resistance battle the cyber-enhanced Neo-facists.*

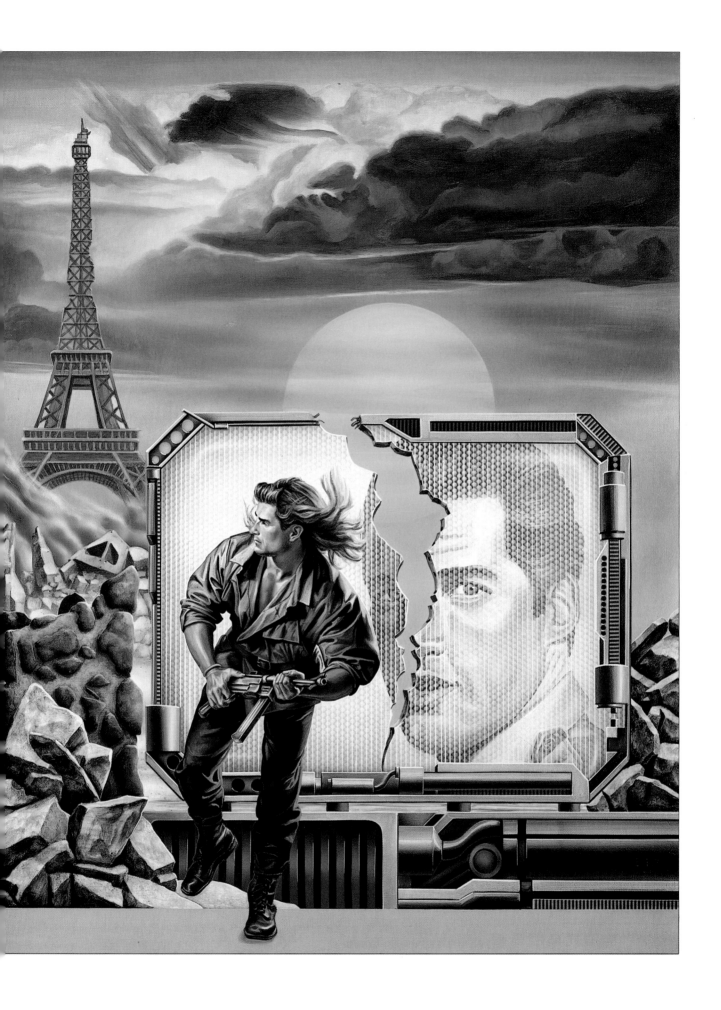

▷ LUNAR APPROACH 1993
Oil on Acrylic
46 x 71 cm (18 x 28 in.)
Commissioned as cover art for Amazing Stories.

▷▷ ASIMOV: VOL.I 1990
Acrylic
92 x 100 cm (36 x 40 in.)
Commissioned as cover art for the 1990
Bantam Books edition of **Isaac Asimov:
The Complete Stories Vol. I**.

*Different elements from the short story collection have
been combined into a single composition.*

△ A CALL TO ARMS 1990
Oil on Acrylic
56 x 92 cm (22 x 36 in.)
Commissioned as cover art for the 1991
Ballantine Books edition of **A Call To Arms**,
by Alan Dean Foster.

▷ THE FALSE MIRROR 1991
Oil on Acrylic
56 x 92 cm (22 x 36 in.)
Commissioned as cover art for the 1992
Ballantine Books edition of **The False Mirror**,
by Alan Dean Foster.

▷▷ THE SPOILS OF WAR 1993
Oil on Acrylic
56 x 76 cm (22 x 30 in.)
Commissioned as cover art for the 1993
Ballantine Books edition of **The Spoils of War**,
by Alan Dean Foster.

THE DAMNED trilogy, by Alan Dean Foster, is given visual continuity among the three books by using a similar cluster of heavily armed figures placed in different settings on each cover. It has been my pleasure to illustrate a number of Alan Dean Foster titles. He is a very visual writer, giving vivid and detailed descriptions of his characters and settings in the text, which is always helpful to the artist.

WORK IN PROGRESS 1993
Mixed Media
122 x 163 x 15 cm (48 x 64 x 6 in.)
Non-commissioned medium relief sculpture, used as interior art in Heavy Metal Pinup Magazine.

△ In progress shots: fitting materials, and spraying with gesso before painting.

▽ Finished piece with external extensions in place.

ORK IN PROGRESS is a piece of art that was total play for this artist. Like its companion piece, Subway Love (see p. 65), it is a medium relief combining my two loves: sculpture and painting. Both works are mixed media constructions, made primarily from discarded styrofoam electronic equipment packing (a wonderful societal symbol) and assorted tubes and fittings. I began by constructing a wood box that would serve as structure and framing for the piece. The different elements were fitted and glued in place. All the materials used, including caulking materials and plaster used to connect forms, are either inert or inert when cured and so should last indefinitely. A canvas covered panel was set into the relief materials for the painted figure(s). When the construction was complete, the entire surface was given a coat of acrylic modelling paste to help unify it and then sprayed with gesso as an undercoating for painting. The painting was done in acrylic, with oil for the figures. Matching texture, colour, perspective and lighting of the surrounding relief in the flat panel was a fine exercise in trompe l'oeil painting.

The scale of a painting is a distinct factor in the impact a work of art has when seen in person. Bigger is not necessarily better, but in this case the larger size is appropriate for the piece. I hope to do similar work in substantially larger scale.

▷ MINING THE OORT 1991
Acrylic
56 x 91 cm (22 x 36 in.)
Commissioned as cover art for the 1992
Ballantine Books edition of **Mining The Oort**,
by Frederick Pohl.

▷▷ ASIMOV: VOL. II 1991
Oil on Acrylic
56 x 91 cm (22 x 36 in.)
Commissioned as cover art for the 1991
Bantam Books edition of **Isaac Asimov:
The Complete Stories Vol. II.**

△ XENOBIA 1978
Acrylic
61 x 91 cm (24 x 36 in.)
Non-commissioned painting.

▽ INDIANA JONES™ 1986
Oil on Acrylic
31 x 40 cm (12 x 16in.)
Unpublished.©1986 Lucas Films Ltd.

▽▽ THE REGENERATION
     OF MAAT 1978
Acrylic
56 x 76 cm (22 x 30 in.)
Non-commissioned painting, used in
Future Life Magazine.

FANTASY & SURREALISM

Most of the art work produced throughout human history could arguably be called Fantasy Art. The archetypal symbolism that has found expression in the art of most cultures through the centuries is found under various guises in contemporary Fantasy Art. While a trend in fine art in the modern era has been to strip representational art of its symbolic content, with varying degrees of success, that content has flourished in other areas of the art world. Fantasy and Science Fiction literature and art have always been a stronghold for that richness of content.

One of the main differences between Surrealist Art and that of the past is that the symbolism of Surrealist Art tends to be specific to the individual artist. Personal symbols may not be directly accessible to others. But, in effective Surrealist Art especially, the personal symbolism of the artist can evoke a response to a more universal symbolism in the viewer, which was the basis of the artist's personal symbols. In my opinion, a lot of the driving force behind effective Fantasy Art comes directly from just such embedded symbolism.

The more successful pieces of my own work, I think, tap into some type of symbolism that speaks well beyond the imagery, and bring about a response in the viewer to those symbols. I do not consciously try to incorporate specific archetypal symbols in my painting or sculpture; they are more a foundation found in the communication language of art itself. A work of art that communicates well with the viewer has successfully transmitted its inherent symbolism.

There are more direct symbols such as dragons or the classic heroic figure of Mr. Jones, pictured on this page. Or the symbolic content can be more subtle, such as the meaning behind flesh which has been painted as cracking and peeling masonry. The latter example is a theme which I have developed into a series of paintings. I am particularly fascinated by the contrasts set up with the use of unexpected materials for certain elements, such as an ideal of feminine beauty, symbol of life and growth, rendered as some kind of inert and corroding material.

◁ IX 1979
Acrylic
25 × 71 cm (10 × 28 in.)
Non-commissioned painting.

▽ Layout sketch for IX; proportions are derived from the golden rectangle.

▷ MEDUSA 1980
Acrylic
46 × 71 cm (18 × 28 in.)
Non-commissioned painting, used as cover art for Science Fiction Chronicle.

△ DREAMS OF DAWN 1988
Acrylic
46 x 71 cm (18 x 28 in.)
Commissioned as cover art for the 1988
Ballantine Books edition of **Dreams Of Dawn**,
by Marti Steussy.

▷ WHERE THE SONG TREES
   GROW 1982
Oil on Acrylic
43 x 62 cm (17 x 24 in.)
Commissioned as cover art for The Magazine
Of Fantasy & Science Fiction.

▷▷ SONGS FROM THE
    DROWNED LANDS 1982
Acrylic
51 x 71 cm (20 x 28 in.)
Commissioned as cover art for the 1983 Ace Books
edition of **Songs From The Drowned Lands**,
by Eileen Kernaghan.

◁ (p. 81) TOYMAN 1981
Oil on Acrylic
46 x 71 cm (18 x 28 in.)
Commissioned as cover art for the 1982 Ace Books
edition of **Toyman**, by E. C. Tubb.

◁◁ THE REGIMENTS OF NIGHT
(p. 80) 1982
Acrylic
46 x 71 cm (18 x 28 in.)
Commissioned as cover art for the 1983 DAW Books
edition of **The Regiments Of Night**, by Brian N. Ball.

A major theme in my work that is evident throughout this volume is the exploration of the contrast between what I think of as the organic and the technological. This contrast is approached in terms of form. I see the technological as having geometric linear elements, which also include curves that are regular and sometimes symmetrical. I see the organic as having free-form and flowing curves, ranging from a wild morass of an uncontrolled liquid splatter to a controlled and flowing living form that has grown for a purpose. An example of this type of contrast would be the concrete distinction between an organic life form and inorganic piece of machinery. But a more subtle contrast can be seen between the graceful fluid forms of the Art Nouveau movement

▷ NIGHT'S MASTER 1984
Acrylic
46 x 66 cm (18 x 26 in.)
Commissioned as cover art for the 1984 Highland
Press edition of **Night's Master**, by Tanith Lee.

▷▷ ORGANIC PERCH 1983
Acrylic
51 x 71 cm (20 x 28 in.)
Commissioned as cover art for Heavy Metal Magazine.

▽ DOOMSTALKER 1984
Acrylic
46 x 71 cm (18 x 28 in.)
Commissioned as cover art for the 1985 Warner
Books edition of **Doomstalker**, by Glen Cook.

and the more rectilinear and geometric curvature of Art Deco forms. Or, it can be seen in the more refined differences between the chiseled hard edged features of the human male figure and the more curvaceous lines of the female form. I love to play with these contrasts as they are embodied by the different elements in my painting and sculpture.

As can be seen in many of the paintings here, I like to take a central theme and develop it in different directions. MEDUSA (see p. 79) and WORK IN PROGRESS (see p. 73) are very similar in subject and symbolic content yet are quite unlike in their visual impact. I appreciate this kind of continuity in other artists' work as well. It is sometimes very exciting throughout the arts to see a single idea pursued and fully developed.

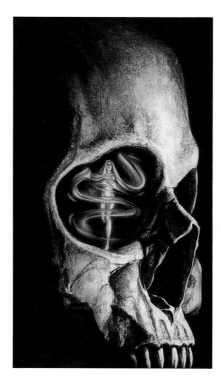

△ CAT'S EYES 1982
Acrylic
38 x 51 cm (15 x 20 in.)
Commissioned as cover art for the 1982
New American Library edition of **Cat's Eyes**,
by Lee Jordan.

▷ SHADOW SINGER 1986
Oil on Acrylic
46 x 71 cm (18 x 28 in.)
Commissioned as cover art for the 1986 Ballantine
Books edition of **Shadow Singer**, by M. J. Bennett.

◁ IN A LONELY PLACE 1982
Acrylic
21 x 33 cm (8 x 13 in.)
Commissioned as cover art for the 1982
Warner Books edition of **In a Lonely Place**,
by Karl Edward Wagoner.
*This is actually a colour sketch that the art director decided
to use as final art. Not always the best policy, but it worked
in this instance.*

△ DR. BLOODMONEY 1984
Acrylic
56 x 71 cm (22 x 28 in.)
Commissioned as cover art for the 1984 Bluejay Books
edition of **Dr. Bloodmoney**, by Philip K. Dick.

▷ THE PENULTIMATE TRUTH 1983
Acrylic
56 x 71 cm (22 x 28 in.)
Commissioned as cover art for the 1983 Bluejay Books
edition of **The Penultimate Truth**, by Philip K. Dick.

▷▷ TIME OUT OF JOINT 1983
Acrylic
56 x 71 cm (22 x 28 in.)
Commissioned as cover art for the 1984 Bluejay Books
edition of **Time Out Of Joint**, by Philip K. Dick.

▷ (p. 90) IMAGE OF THE BEAST 1984
Oil on Acrylic
46 x 71 cm (18 x 28 in.)
Commissioned as cover art for the 1983 Ace Books
edition of **Image Of The Beast**, by Philip José Farmer.

▷▷ THE REMAKING
(p. 91) OF SIGMUND FREUD 1984
Oil on Acrylic
46 x 71 cm (18 x 28 in.)
Commissioned as cover art for the 1985 Ace Books
edition of **The Remaking Of Sigmund Freud**,
by Barry N. Malzberg.

Philip K. Dick is one of my favourite authors. His story lines, and general take on life for that matter, are wonderfully offbeat and quite unique. That being the case I jumped at the opportunity to do covers for a number of his titles for Bluejay Books. Since his work leans heavily toward the conceptual end of the literary spectrum, I thought a more conceptual approach to the cover art would be appropriate. I also borrowed a lick from The Ellison Series and incorporated a likeness of Philip K. Dick in each painting. I picked up on some of his general themes, such as time displacement and post-nuclear worlds, and made compositions that were specific to each book. Some projects are fun from the reading of the manuscript phase through to the final painting, and these covers were just that.

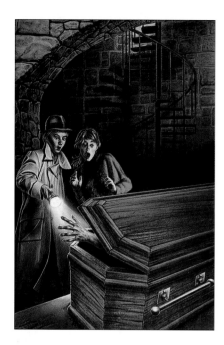

△△ VISITING VAMPIRE 1988
Acrylic
46 x 71 cm (18 x 28 in.)
Commissioned as cover art for the 1988
Simon & Schuster edition of **Visiting Vampire**,
by Drew Stevenson.

△ THE MONSTER'S RING 1987
Acrylic
46 x 71 cm (18 x 28 in.)
Commissioned as cover art for the 1987
Simon & Schuster edition of **The Monster's Ring**,
by Bruce Coville.

△ THE CREEP 1985
Acrylic
46 x 71 cm (18 x 28 in.)
Commissioned as cover art for the 1986 Simon &
Schuster edition of **The Creep**, by Susan Dodson.
This Painting was altered from its published form: a
threatened young girl was replaced by a pet dragon.
Noted illustrator Kevin Johnson modeled for The Creep –
no value judgement implied.

▷ BEST OF E. F. RUSSELL 1985
Acrylic
46 x 71 cm (18 x 28 in.)
Commissioned as cover art for the 1986 Ballantine
Books edition of **The Best Of Eric Frank Russell**.

△ Tarzan series concept sketch.

▷ TARZAN THE APE MAN 1989
Acrylic
86 × 100 cm (34 × 39 in.)
© 1990 Edgar Rice Burroughs, Inc. All rights reserved.
Commissioned as cover art for the 1990
Ballantine Books edition of **Tarzan The Ape Man**,
by Edgar Rice Burroughs.
Reprinted by permission of Ballantine Books.

▽ Medium relief sculptural approach to the series,
rejected due to time considerations.

While I was growing up, Tarzan, by that time an inter-generational icon of popular culture, was standard fare in books, comics, and Saturday morning television. I discovered some of my favourite artists while perusing the pages of different Tarzan tales; so the assignment to illustrate the first six Tarzan books was an unqualified honour. It did present a challenge, however. How would I adapt my style to fit the subject matter, and what approach would set my work off from the volumes of work that preceded it?

My first thought was to do a series of low relief painting/sculptures, combining two of my interests and producing something definitely unique. The time required to produce the small dimensional sample to the left, however, made it clear to me that the execution of full sized dimensional paintings was out of the question. The long approval process involved in a tightly held property like Tarzan, left me with about one week for execution of each painting, half the painting time usually allotted.

I did retain some of the concepts behind the dimensional approach in the final series concept. This was done by employing the unifying concepts of extreme downward perspective, exaggerating dimensionality, and most directly in the use of break-outs from the image area that extended into the type area. These two design elements established continuity for the series.

▷ THE BEASTS OF TARZAN 1989
Acrylic
86 x 100 cm (34 x 39 in.)
© 1990 Edgar Rice Burroughs, Inc. All rights reserved.
Commissioned as cover art for the 1990
Ballantine Books edition of **The Beasts Of Tarzan**,
by Edgar Rice Burroughs.
Reprinted by permission of Ballantine Books.

▷▷ THE RETURN OF TARZAN 1989
Acrylic
86 x 100 cm (34 x 39 in.)
© 1990 Edgar Rice Burroughs, Inc. All rights reserved.
Commissioned as cover art for the 1990
Ballantine Books edition of **The Return Of Tarzan**,
by Edgar Rice Burroughs.
Reprinted by permission of Ballantine Books.

These covers were done before I discovered computer modelling. Working out the drawings with this type of extreme perspective would have been greatly assisted by constructing a simplified version of the scene in the computer and using that view for drawing reference. There is a tendency to think that the more uniform results achieved when using mechanical tools, such as the airbrush or computer, tend to obscure the individual style of the artist. I have found to the contrary that there are so many variables involved in the creation of a work of art, that the artist's style will come through regardless of the tools used.

△ JUNGLE TALES OF TARZAN 1990
Acrylic
86 x 100 cm (34 x 39 in.)
© 1990 Edgar Rice Burroughs, Inc. All rights reserved.
Commissioned as cover art for the 1990
Ballantine Books edition of **Jungle Tales Of Tarzan**,
by Edgar Rice Burroughs.

▷ TARZAN AND THE
   JEWELS OF OPAR 1990
Acrylic
86 x 100 cm (34 x 39 in.)
© 1990 Edgar Rice Burroughs, Inc. All rights reserved.
Commissioned as cover art for the 1990 Ballantine
Books edition of **Tarzan And The Jewels Of Opar**,
by Edgar Rice Burroughs.

▷▷ SON OF TARZAN 1989
Acrylic
86 x 100 cm (34 x 39 in.)
© 1990 Edgar Rice Burroughs, Inc. All rights reserved.
Commissioned as cover art for the 1990
Ballantine Books edition of **Son Of Tarzan**,
by Edgar Rice Burroughs.

All above images are reprinted by permission
of Ballantine Books.

△ ALTERNATE PRESIDENTS 1991
Acrylic
46 x 71 cm (18 x 28 in.)
Commissioned as cover art for the 1991 TOR
Books edition of **Alternate Presidents**, edited
by Mike Resnick.

▷ ALTERNATE WARRIORS 1992
Acrylic
46 x 71 cm (18 x 28 in.)
Commissioned as cover art for the 1993 TOR Books
edition of **Alternate Warriors**, edited by Mike Resnick.

▷▷ RINN'S STAR 1990
Acrylic
46 x 71 cm (18 x 28 in.)
Commissioned as cover art for the 1990 Ballantine
Books edition of **Rinn's Star**, by Paula E. Downing.

▽ ALTERNATE KENNEDYS 1991
Mixed Media
46 x 71 cm (18 x 28 in.)
Commissioned as cover art for the 1992 TOR
Books edition of **Alternate Kennedys**, edited
by Mike Resnick.

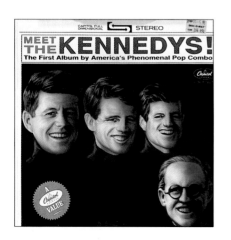

The entertaining imagery for the "Alternate Series", edited by Mike Resnick, was the result of creative brainstorming by TOR Book's editor Patrick Nielsen Hayden. When Patrick first called asking for a painting that reverses the famous "DEWEY DEFEATS TRUMAN" photo, my first thought was that here is someone who enjoys his job. This assessment proved itself true by the following assignments: a takeoff on the MEET THE BEATLES album cover art and Ghandi depicted as Rambo. That sort of fun easily spills over to make the illustrator's job entertaining too.

▷ THE BRADBURY CHRONICLES 1991
Acrylic
46 x 71 cm (18 x 28 in.)
Originally commissioned as cover art for the Phantasia
Press hard cover edition of **The Bradbury Chronicles**,
edited by Wm. H. Nolan and Martin H. Greenburg.

*Unfortunately, no industry is immune to the legal vagaries
of the business world, and publishing is certainly no
exception. Phantasia Press lost the publication rights to
the book and this painting was never published.*

▷ EURYDICE 1989
Acrylic
76 x 127 cm (30 x 50 in.)
Non-commissioned painting, used as cover art for
the 1990 Ballantine Books edition of **Megagnomes**,
by Alan Dean Foster.

◁ GROUNDTIES 1991
Acrylic
46 x 71 cm (18 x 28 in.)
Commissioned as cover art for the 1991 Warner
Books edition of **Groundties**, by Jane S. Fancher.

▽ UPLINK 1991
Acrylic
46 x 71 cm (18 x 28 in.)
Commissioned as cover art for the 1992 Warner
Books edition of **Uplink**, by Jane S. Fancher.

▷ FULL SPECTRUM III 1990

Acrylic

76 x 100 cm (30 x 40 in.)

Commissioned as cover art for the 1991 Bantam Books
edition of **Full Spectrum III**, edited by Lou Aronica,
Amy Stout, and Betsy Mitchell.

*Elements from different stories in the collection are combined
in a single composition.*

▷ MACHINERIES OF JOY 1988
Oil on Acrylic
71 x 38 cm (28 x 15 in.)
Commissioned as cover art for the 1989 Bantam Books,
USA mass market edition of **Machineries of Joy**,
by Ray Bradbury.

MACHINERIES OF JOY is the first in a number of paintings that were commissioned to illustrate short story collections, in which I took a different approach to developing a cover solution. The art director for Bantam Books, Jamie Warren Youll (married to Steve Youll, a British born artist who is one of the stellar talents in the field), called with an illustrator's dream assignment: not only to do a painting for a short story collection by the classic Science Fiction author Ray Bradbury, but to paint what ever image I chose! Having grown up with these stories, the opportunity to illustrate them was a true privilege.

The painting is actually a composite of various elements culled from different stories in the collection, similar to a montage, but combined into a single unified composition. The resulting image stands alone

not only as a wonderfully surrealistic juxtaposition of seemingly unrelated elements, but also as a valid illustration of the text. Being quite pleased with the resulting painting, I have often taken this approach in other projects where the art director was open to something unusual. Other examples include ASIMOV VOL. I (see p. 69), ASIMOV VOL. II (see p. 75), and the two preceding spreads: THE BRADBURY CHRONICLES and FULL SPECTRUM III.

Jamie assigned each title in the Bradbury series to a different illustrator, with the same parameters (none); a true act of courage. The series, unified by her excellent type design, was a spectacular success, and a credit to all involved.

▷ (p. 110-111) MERCYCLE 1991
Oil on Acrylic
76 x 100 cm (30 x 40 in.)
Commissioned as cover art for the 1992 Berkley Books mass market edition of **Mercycle**, by Piers Anthony.

The psychedelic variety of sea life around the coral reef is a perfect subject for artists like myself who appreciate wild colour and form.

△ WAY STATION 1992
Acrylic
31 x 36 cm (12 x 14 in.)
Commissioned as cover art for the 1993 Macmillan
trade edition of **Way Station**, by Clifford D. Simak.

*In the text a farmhouse was actually a transporter gateway
to the rest of the galaxy.*

◁ MERMAID 1991
Oil on Acrylic
76 x 112 cm (30 x 46 in.)
A non-commissioned painting.

△ EMPIRE OF THE ATOM 1992
Acrylic
38 x 46 cm (15 x 18 in.)
Commissioned for the 1992 Macmillan trade edition
of **Empire of the Atom**, by A. E. Van Vogt.

▷ BLACK TRUMP 1994
Oil on Acrylic
76 x 57 cm (30 x 22.5 in.)
Commissioned for the 1995 Baen Books mass market
edition of **Wild Cards: Black Trump**, edited by
George R. R. Martin.

The very popular WILD CARDS series edited by George R. R. Martin posed an interesing challenge: to present the various mutant characters and normal characters with special powers within a consistent series format. Armed with character descriptions provided by the editor, George Martin, I used the graphic element of a fanned

deck of cards as a title tie-in as well as a frame that would contain different characters and would also suggest a series of scenes from the short story collection. The design phase of this series lent itself perfectly to the computer. The ease with which elements can be created, moved and adjusted electronically make it a natural addition to any artist's studio.

△ CARDSHARKS 1992
Oil on Acrylic
76 × 57 cm (30 × 22.5 in.)
Commissioned for the 1992 Baen Books mass market
edition of **Wild Cards: Cardsharks**, edited by
George R. R. Martin.

◁◁ (p. 116-117) MARKED CARDS 1993
Oil on Acrylic
71 × 53 cm (28 × 21 in.)
Commissioned for the 1993 Baen Books mass market
edition of **Wild Cards: Marked Cards**, edited by
George R. R. Martin.

The two paintings RIVER OF TIME and SONG OF CECILIA were painted consecutively, and are similar in look and atmosphere since the one gave rise to the other. I began the design phase of the painting RIVER OF TIME by experiment with the use of a three dimensional computer modelling program to develop the drawing of the temple. In these programs a model of the proposed scene is actually built piece by piece in the computer. Those elements are then placed and arranged in a scene. Textures are applied to all the various objects or elements within the scene. Lighting sources are established, and finally a virtual camera is placed in the scene to take a "snapshot" from the desired perspective. One can quickly determine what impact changes in lighting or placement of elements would have on the overall composition, and can easily play with any aspect to achieve the desired results, or to discover something unexpected. In this case, the design for the latter painting was developed while tinkering with elements of the former. The final computer generated image can be used as reference for the finished painting, as it was for these two paintings, or as the finished art, depending on the artist's requirements.

▷▷ (p. 120-121) SONG OF CECILIA 1994
Oil on Acrylic
92 × 62 cm (36 × 24 in.)
A non-commissioned painting.

This painting contains some obscured imagery: a sea horse,
turtle, dolphin, dragon, and Neptune.

▷ RIVER OF TIME 1994
Oil on Acrylic
43 × 97 cm (17 × 38 in.)
Commissioned for the 1994 Bantam Books mass
market edition of **River of Time**, by David Brin.

▽ POSITRONIC MAN 1993
Electronic File
A computer reworking of **I Have No Mouth**
(see p. 25), commissioned by The Doubleday Book
& Music Club.

▽▽ Another variation, based on the same painting.
These pieces began with a scan of an existing piece of art.
The scan was altered in a photo manipulation programme,
with a painted figure added in the upper piece and computer
generated spheres added in the lower.

FUTURE MEDIA

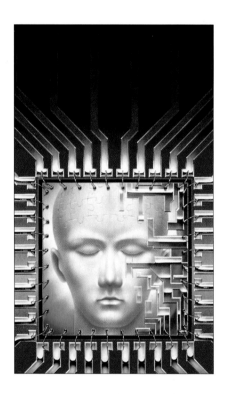

The choice of media an artist makes for a work of art is always appropriate if it enables the artist to achieve the results desired. This certainly applies to art created with the ever expanding repertoire of tools developed by the current explosion in computer science technology. Within the past ten years, the graphic arts have been completely transformed by the computer. Virtually all page layout, image and typesetting, colour separations etc., which used to be done on paper or film, are now done electronically. This is expanding to include all types of image generation, from traditional photography and illustration, to new avenues of expression only possible through the use of the new technology.

The revolution in computer generated art is now in its infancy, but one can easily see that it will quickly take its place alongside traditional media as the programs become more sophisticated and as artists become adept at using them. Economics alone will make computer generated art commonplace in publishing. Artwork can be created, altered if necessary, placed in a page layout, colour separated, and sent to press without ever leaving the electronic domain. This eliminates many costs of production and reduces labour costs as well. The economics of mimicry will play an inevitable role, for better or worse. The commercial music field has already been dramatically changed by the fact that a good musician with a synthesizer can produce end results that are virtually indistinguishable from what a full hired orchestra would produce, and at a fraction of the cost. Similarly, one in-house computer artist may be able to take over the production of a number of freelance artists, and at similar savings to the publication. Happily, it is the tools that are changing; artistic talent will always be in demand. Even if demand for artists is decreased in some areas by technology, the expansion in venue created by that technology will, if anything, increase the overall demand for art and artists.

Electronic painting will never replace traditional painting, nor is it intended to. The computer is simply a new tool. A problem does arise for computer generated painting, however, within the context of the established gallery system for selling original art and reproductions. That is: "What is the original art?" Which raises the question: "What is art?" My college sculpture professor, for whom I still have the highest regard, did a lot of work with rope, fibres and cable. In some of his pieces, rope and cables would be suspended from the ceiling with the ends carefully coiled on the floor. I was recently walking past a SoHo gallery in New York City, and noticed a lot of ropes and cables hanging from the walls and ceiling of the gallery space. Thinking it might be the work of my former instructor, I walked in and asked the woman behind the desk who the artist was. She

looked at me speculatively, then said: "We are in between shows, sir."

So, bypassing the question "what is art?"; in the case of a digital painting, is the original art the electronic file, or some type of output from that file? Or would that be considered a print? To sell an original work of art, would an electronic file be presented, allowing the purchaser to output the image? Could the purchaser then have a number of prints made and sell those prints? Or should a print or some type of output be made from the file for sale, and the file itself destroyed? And what about differences in quality and permanence among output devices? Also, if a file is altered slightly, at what point does it become a completely new image in the eyes of the copyright laws? Again, it beats me. But I assume these issues and others will be resolved in the marketplace in much the same manner that photography as fine art settled out.

The response among my peers to this new technology is quite interesting. Some have picked up the banner (or scanner) with an evangelical fervour. Others couldn't be less interested. I find myself somewhere in

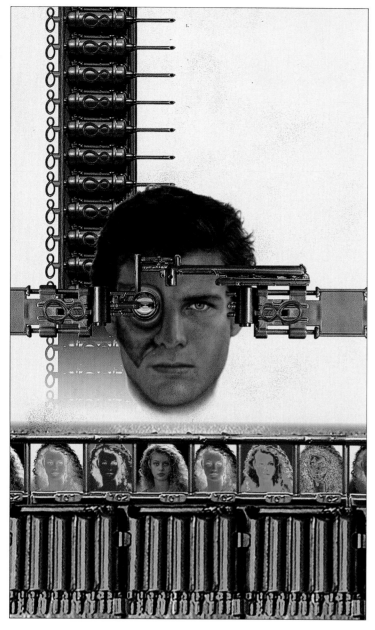

the middle, finding that the computer has become a fascinating and indispensable tool in my studio, while not feeling the slightest inclination to abandon traditional media in favour of it. It is the variety of experience using the different tools that I personally love. Using a brush and paint on canvas is a completely different experience from delving into a new 3D world that one can generate digitally, which again is different from the tactile feel of sculpting in clay (or styrofoam, for that matter). And all of it is great fun!

The various media interact nicely as well. The computer can be used in designing a canvas painting; sculpture can be used as reference for painting; a sculpture and its environment can be developed using computer modelling before the actual sculpture is made; and painting, sculpture and photography can be scanned and incorporated in digital imagery. All this can be integrated with the motion and sound capabilities of digital media, creating new and limitless possibilities. The current generation of art students will mature with digital media as a standard part of their curriculum. This is nothing but good news for the art world as a whole, in my opinion, and I expect great things to come.

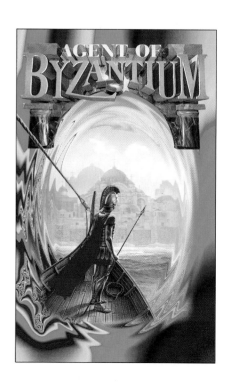

▷ CLAW ISLAND 1994
Electronic File
Commissioned by Parker Brothers for a game board.
This piece was created entirely in a 3D program. Each element in the scene was modelled according to a general layout provided by the client. Each element was then placed in the scene with different textures assigned to each surface or object. Different light sources were placed in the scene, as was a virtual camera that would take a "snapshot" of the scene from the desired angle. Once everything was set, it took my relatively powerful (for 1994) Macintosh computer five days to render the image.

△ DOWN THE HATCH 1995
Mixed Media
A non-commissioned computer designed medium
relief painting/sculpture.